THE

WESTERN STATES:

THEIR PURSUITS AND POLICY.

BY

Dr. WILLIAM ELDER.

PHILADELPHIA:
RINGWALT & BROWN, STEAM-POWER PRINTERS,
Nos. 111 and 113 South Fourth Street.
June, 1865.

THE WESTERN STATES:

THEIR PURSUITS AND POLICY.

Products and Pursuits.

That portion of the Mississippi valley which is drained by the Ohio, Mississippi and Missouri rivers, and embraced in the States of Ohio, Indiana, Illinois, Missouri, Kentucky, Wisconsin, Iowa, Michigan, Minnesota, Kansas, and the *territory* of Nebraska, lies all above the 36th degree of north latitude, and is well distinguished by its characteristics and capabilities from the States, East, South and West of it. These States take the rank of agricultural, as distinguished from the planting, gold-bearing, and mixed industrial regions which surround them. They are almost the youngest of the sisterhood, and being eminently fitted for farming industry, the cultivation of the soil was necessarily the earliest stage of their industrial history. Hitherto their growth has been in this direction to such extent and with such success, that they are regarded and distinguished as agricultural states. By this loose general classification, however, we must not assume to settle their policy, determine their enterprise, or foreclose their prospects. If the designation were used only to describe the earliest phase of their productions and pursuits, it would be correct enough; to indicate their rank among the other States, it is proper enough; used inclusively, it is accurate enough; but used exclusively, it is manifestly and greatly erroneous. They have some manufacturing industry, and they have some commercial relations with the rest of the Union and with foreign nations, and they are capable of great enlargement in both respects.

It is our purpose to examine their condition and prospects in all these aspects. Our data are derived from the agricultural volume of the Census Report of 1860; the preliminary Census Report for the same year on their manufactures; the Reports of the Agricultural Department at Washington, the Treasury Reports upon commerce and navigation, and for a special purpose, the Report of the Commissioner of Internal Revenue for the year 1864.*

Population and Property—Amount and Proportion.

The aggregate population of these eleven valley States in 1860, was 10,445,580—33½ per cent of the total population of the Union. Their real and personal property was valued at $4,519,263,737,—31.87 per cent of the total wealth of the nation, slaves excluded. The cash value of their farms was $2,462,350,921,—37.05 per cent of the total. In farming implements and machinery they had $80,275,535,—32 per cent., and of live stock $382,405,994,—35.1 per cent of the whole.

Thus in population, and in property connected with husbandry, they stood within a trifle, over or under, of one-third of the Union in each item.

---

*The fiscal year ending June 30, 1860, is chosen as better and fairer for the purposes of this inquiry than any other, or any average of years, for several reasons: It is the year immediately preceding the rebellion, and fully closed before our domestic business or foreign trade was in any wise affected by that event. It was a year of fair prices. Our exports and imports were larger than in any that preceded it. Previous to the year 1854 our domestic exports, exclusive of specie, had never reached the value of two hundred millions of dollars. Their average value during the six years immediately preceding 1860 was 247 millions; in 1860 they mounted to 316 millions, being 38 millions higher than the highest ever before attained. It is the year to which the Eighth Census closely applies in the matter of domestic productions; moreover the business of that year, both productive and commercial, may be taken to have fully recovered from the disturbance of 1857, and had not reached the stage of inflation. All the conditions were as nearly normal and as even an index of our capacities as any in our business history.

Agricultural Products, value and proportion in 1859.

Kind.	*Quantity.*		*Proportion to product of the nation.*
Wheat,	102,398,994	bushels,	59.1 per cent.
Indian Corn,	470,190,097	"	56.0 "
Rye,	5,160,418	"	24.4 "
Oats,	67,567,707	"	39.1 "
Tobacco,	173,758,747	pounds,	40.0 "
Wool,	25,231,830	"	41.8 "
Slaughtered Animals	$81,800,333		34.8 "
Hay,	7,219,957	tons,	37.8 "
Butter,	164,785,997	lbs.,	35.8 "
Irish Potatoes,	36,759,801	bushels,	33.2 "
Wine,	955,717	gallons,	59.0 "
Hemp,	67,555	tons,	90.7 "

Of the total value of all the agricultural products of the year, including twenty-five other items of less importance than those enumerated here, these States produced $1,159,605,660, which was equal to 39.7 per cent of the total of the Union, exclusive of cotton, rice, cane sugar and molasses. Thus it appears that with a capital of real and personal property something less than thirty-two per cent, they reached forty per cent of the farming products proper of the Union in the year 1859.

Products for Market and Home Consumption.

We strike from the aggregate the estimated value of the farming implements, horses, mules, working oxen, milch cows, held for use, $259,605,660, which leaves 900 millions worth, for immediate consumption by the producing States, and for market in the other States and in foreign countries.

Foreign Market for the Year's Crop.

The United States exported in the year ending June 30, 1860, to all foreign countries, of the articles enumerated and embraced in the preceding statements, the value of $61,891,042. It is impossible to trace these exports to the several States in which they were produced, blended as they are at the ports of shipment, but as they are all articles in domestic use, and in nearly equal proportions to population in all the States, we may safely assume for the Western States a proportion of the exports equal to their share in the production. This, as before stated, is 39.7 per cent. We will, for convenience, take it at 40, which would give a foreign market for $24,800,000 of the value of all agricultural articles. Subtract this from the sum of the disposable crop of the year, and we have for the consumption of the producing States, and the market of the other States, the value of $875,200,000.

A foreign market for 2¾ per cent. and a reserve of 97¼ of the crop, or as $1 is to $35.36 worth.

Market for the Produce of the Western States in the other States.

By the following process we endeavor to obtain an estimate of the market which the eleven Western States had in the other States of the Union for these products of the year 1859.

The value of all these articles produced, in all the States, was $2,918,617,192; reduced by an equal proportion for farming utensils and live stock not on sale, or retained for use as agents in further production, as allowed for in the Western States, leaves a total of disposable value of $2,169,431,833. The total exports to foreign countries of these commodities was 62 millions. The balance left for domestic consumption would be $2,107,431,833. The consumers for these, were a national population of 31 millions, of which the Western States had 33½ per cent. Their proportion of the total home consumption would be $684,915,345, leaving them a surplus demanding a market in the other States amounting to $190,284,655. *A market in the other States for more than seven and a half times the value of the exports to all foreign countries; or,* 20,702,467 *inhabitants of the other States of the Union afford them a market average per capita of* $9.19, *while about seventy-two millions of European customers in manufacturing countries, took an average of* 17¼ *cents worth per capita, or* $12,400,000 *in all, the other* $12,400,000 *going to countries in Asia, Africa and America, which supply us with unmanufactured articles.*

Distribution among the other States Explained.

The 10 Southern Slave States, (Texas not included,) which needed these supplies, had a total population of 8,499,118, of whom 3,338,544 were slaves, who may be taken to consume much less than the average quantity of western produce assigned to them, but a glance at the agricultural productions of the New England States will show that to make up their ratio of consumption they would require as much more than they produce as would cover the deficit of the Slave States; we may, therefore, take the average demand for supplies from the Western States to be a safe approximation to the actual total which we obtain by the process here adopted. The United States consume very exactly five bushels of wheat, or one barrel of flour, per head per annum. New York and New England in 1860, together required twenty-six millions of bushels in addition to their own production to make up their consumption. Here then there is a market for eleven millions of bushels more than the average adopted assigns to the share of the slaves, if they consumed not a grain of the breadstuffs. Thus we measure the total market in the other states safely enough without distributing it with particular accuracy.

A Home Consumption provided for the total Exports to Manufacturing Countries.

The countries in Europe from which we import manufactured goods, took of the produce of the Western States in 1860 to the value of $12,400,000. How many immigrants from those countries, if located in these states, would have consumed this amount? At $65.66½ per capita, it would have required only 188,837 persons; certainly not more than the number of immigrants which these states usually receive in the course of a year. What number of immigrants from the manufacturing countries with which we trade would consume 12$\frac{4}{10}$ millions worth of western produce, if located in any of the other states? At $9.19 a head it would take 1,349,292. But if only 150,000 immigrants a year should enter the mining regions west of these states, they would take at least 7½ of the 12$\frac{4}{10}$ millions worth for which their countrymen at home are customers; 50,000 locating in these states would take 3¼ millions worth, and 180,000 in the Old States would make a market for the balance. Is this too much to expect or to count upon with confidence? Is it not much below the probabilities of a well adapted policy?

The relative value of a home to a foreign market is obvious; and as a question of commerce merely, may be instantly decided upon the facts. We are now led a step farther for the fuller consideration of the subject thus opened.

The Foreign Market for United States Produce.

This branch of the inquiry is not a mere process of ciphering in pursuit of that absurd thing called "the balance of trade," a fancied gain or loss ascertained by custom-house valuations, and expressed in arithmetical figures. The official reports of the commerce of Great Britain for the eleven years next preceding 1864, show a total of imports amounting to 2,061 millions of pounds sterling, and a total of exports of only 1,308 millions of pounds. Did she lose 753 millions of pounds by the business? Did she lose 36½ per cent on her ventures, or did she make a clean profit of 57½ per cent by them?

On the other hand, the exports of the United States in the 11 years next preceding 1864, exceeded the imports by 80½ millions. Did we lose or gain these 80½ millions? Does England grow rich upon the excess of her imports and we upon the excess of our exports? These figures mean nothing. The balance of trade is not in the official values exchanged, because the real values are always even when the merchants' accounts are settled. It is in the kind and course of foreign commerce that the results tell. This, therefore, is the object of our present inquiry.

In the following tabular statement the countries which supply us with manufactured articles are distinguished from "all other countries," with the intention of distinguishing the kinds of trade we have with them respectively. By "manufacturing countries" we mean the British and French dominions in Europe, Hamburg, Bremen and all German countries, and Holland and Belgium, which send us all the manufactures worth considering for the purpose in hand. "All other countries," embrace all others in the Eastern hemisphere and in America, which supply us with tropical, or semi-tropical and other raw products;—the products of the former countries competing with our own manufacturing industry, those of the latter ministering to it, or affording us commodities which our own climate and soil do not produce, and which are not manufactured further than preservation and transportation require.

Domestic Exports of the United States in the year 1859-60.

To all Countries.	*To Manufacturing Countries.*	*To "all other Countries."*
BREADSTUFFS AND PROVISIONS, (STRICTLY.)		
$38,858,086	$13,952,988=36 p. c.	$24,905,098=64 p. c.
OTHER AGRICULTURAL PRODUCTS, (14 CLASSES.)		
8,471,323	5,279,586=62.3 p. c.	3,191,737=37.7 p. c.
$47,329,409	$19,232,574=40.6 p. c.	$28,096,835=59.4 p. c.
LEAF TOBACCO.		
15,906,547	12,238,791=77 p. c.	3,667,756=23 p. c.
$63,235,956*	$31,471,365=49.8 p. c.	$31,764,591=50.2 p. c.
MANUFACTURED ARTICLES.		
$39,803,080	$7,871,970=19.75 p. c.	$31,931,110=80.25p.c.
SPECIE.—FOREIGN AND DOMESTIC.		
$66,546,239	$59,276,340=89 p. c.	$7,269,899=11 p. c.

Raw cotton to the value of $190,000,000 went to the countries which we designate "manufacturing," and $1,000,000 worth went to Mexico. The export of rice, was six-tenths to South America and the West Indies, and four-tenths to manufacturing Europe. The tobacco, of which the total export is here given, was produced, 40 per cent in the Western States, 4¼ per cent in the New England, Middle and Pacific States, and 55¾ per cent in the rebel States.

This classification of the kinds of our domestic exports and of the foreign customers will best teach its lessons after looking at the kinds of imports we receive in exchange from each class of these customers.

FOREIGN IMPORTS OF THE FISCAL YEAR 1859-60.

Total.	From manufacturing countries.	From all other countries.
$362,166,254	$208,707,314=57.6 per cent.	$153,458,940=42.4 per cent.

*This total is $1,346,914 greater than the previously stated total value of our agricultural products, which may be accounted for by a corresponding difference between the export prices and census valuations.

Character of the Foreign Imports from Non-manufacturing Countries.

The imports from countries other than those which send us manufactures, it is seen, amounted to 42.4 per cent, or nearly $\frac{7}{16}$ of the total. They consisted of such articles as sugar, molasses, spices, saltpetre, india-rubber, indigo and other dye-stuffs, fruits, wool under 20 cts. a pound, and coarser than our climate produces, cocoa, tea, coffee, mahogany and other tropical woods, gums, medicines, guano, hides, grasses, tobacco and cigars of tropical or semi-tropical origin, and $8,402,948 of specie, leaving a balance of foreign specie imported from all manufacturing countries of $147,187 only.

Character of Imports from Manufacturing Countries.

The kinds or classes of these imports, exceeding a quarter of a million dollars in value, were, generally stated, acids, bleaching powders, clocks and watches, clothing, coal, cotton manufactures, dolls and toys, dressed furs, hats and bonnets, iron, steel, laces and embroideries, lead, gloves, tanned and dressed skins, sole and upper leather, linseed, hempseed and essential oils, paints, paper, printed books, salt, silk piece goods and hosiery, soda, brandy, spirits, wines, chinaware, and manufactures of cotton, wool and worsted, flax, glass, gold and silver, hemp, iron and steel, lead, leather, paper, wood and zinc.

Of these manufactures, with others of less value, but belonging to the same class of goods, amounting in the aggregate value to 202½ millions, we had from Great Britain, 135½ millions; from France, 41½ millions, from Germany and Belgium, 23 millions, and from Spain, 2½ millions. The woolen, cotton, hemp, iron and steel, silk and flax manufactures, imported that year and retained for consumption, amounted to 124¼ millions; the ready-made clothing to 2 millions; salt and coal, 2 millions; total of these articles 128 millions, from countries which took in the same year of our agricultural and manufactured products, other than raw cotton, 39⅓ millions, and of our specie 59½ millions.

Resumé of kind and course of our Foreign Trade.

The manufacturing countries of Europe sent us 203 millions worth of such goods as competed with our own industries, and took in exchange of our agricultural products, manufactures and Northern tobacco, 32 millions; raw cotton, 190 millions; Southern leaf tobacco, 7⅓ millions, and 59½ millions of our specie. Total in these items, 289 millions—excess of our exports to, over imports from them, 86 millions.

The non-manufacturing countries took of our agricultural exports, 28 millions; of our leaf tobacco, 3⅜ millions; of our manufactures, 32 millions, and of our specie 7¼ millions; a total of 71 millions. Our total imports from them for the year amounted to 156½ millions, an excess of 85½ millions, for which they drew upon us in favor of the manufacturing countries.

To them, in general statement, we sent 64 per cent of our breadstuffs and provisions; 59.4 per cent of our total agricultural products, exclusive of tobacco; 50.3 per cent of our total, including tobacco, or half our raw products, and of our manufactures four-fifths, while they took one million less of specie than they sent us. Of the total imports of the year, they sent us 42.4 per cent, or 7/16 directly, with many millions more indirectly, through the hands of British, French and other European merchants.

Thus stands our trade with all non-manufacturing countries. We add a brief general view of our trade in the same year with the Continent of America, and the adjacent islands of the Atlantic and Pacific Oceans.

Our imports of the productions of the climates North and South of us in the Western hemisphere, amounted to $111,-555,562, of which $37,570,645 was in sugar and raw hides, which, so far from competing with our own articles of the same kind, only supplied our deficient product. $4,862,690 worth of the leaf and manufactured tobacco of the West Indies and South America supplied a different kind or quality, displacing our own only as silks displace calicoes. All the other imports except those admitted under the Reciprocity Treaty with the British North American possessions, were simply supplementary to our own commodities, or were material for our manufactures. Our total exports to these American countries amounted to $70,687,781, leaving us 41 millions to pay through our European mercantile factors.

Manufactures in the Western States.

The third volume of the Census of 1860 is not yet published, and we have not at command such fulness and completeness of details in the branch of manufactures as we could wish, but in the Preliminary Report, published in 1862, a digest of all the data is given, which sufficiently serves our purpose. Of the twenty-eight classes of manufactures, mining and mechanic products given in the "Preliminary Report," we take twenty-four for presentment here, rejecting only anthracite coal, of which the Western States have none, illuminating gas, which has no reference to commerce, and salt and fish, in which none of the conditions of fair comparison of manufacturing enterprise can be found; but the manufacture of musical instruments, india rubber goods, jewelry and silver-ware are admitted, because these are possible in the Western States, though as yet wholly produced in the Eastern. The twenty-four classes selected are, agricultural implements, pig iron, bar and other rolled iron, steam engines and machinery, iron founding, bituminous coal, lead, copper, printed books, jobs and newspapers, sewing machines, clothing, sawed and planed lumber, flour and meal, spirituous liquors, malt liquors, cotton, woolen and mixed, leather, boots and shoes, india rubber goods, furniture, musical instruments, jewelry and silver-ware, and soap and candles.

In all these kinds of manufacturing and producing industry, other than those belonging to the rivers and oceans, the forests, and the four classes above excepted, the condition and progress of the Western States is measured by those of the Eastern and Middle States, by which general designation is meant the six New England States, and the States of New York, New Jersey, Pennsylvania, Delaware, Maryland, and the District of Columbia.

Value of the Products of Twenty-four classes of Mining, Manufacturing and Mechanic Arts, as given in the Preliminary Census of 1860, and the Compendium of 1850.

Year 1860, 11 Western States,	$217,476,446
" 1850, " " "	105,461,612
Increase in 10 years, (106.2 p. c.)	$112,014,834
Year 1860, 12 New England and Middle States,	$703,255,086
" 1850, " " "	432,044,209
Increase in 10 years, (62.7 p. c.)	$271,210,877

In addition to the detailed statements from which these deductions are made, the Superintendent of the Census gives, for the purpose of embracing other manufactures not stated in detail, "Approximate Statistics of the Products of Industry for the year ending June 1, 1860." In the Compendium of 1850 we have the corresponding totals. They stand in the two groups of states here compared, thus:

Approximate Value of all Products of Mining, Mechanics and Manufactures.

Year 1860. Eleven Western States,	$390,411,942
" 1850. " " "	171,022,976
Increase in ten years (128.2 per cent.),	$219,388,966
Year 1860. Twelve New England and Middle States,	$1,298,207,058
" 1850. " " "	746,715,814
Increase in ten years (73.8 per cent.),	$551,491,244

Depending upon the probable accuracy of the Superintendent's "Approximate Statement," we take it as the juster exhibition for the purpose of comparison, because the minor or less considerable forms of manufactures are those in which the younger States exceed the same kinds in the older States, and should be included.

These industrial products of the eleven Western States in 1850 bore the proportion of 22.9 per cent to those of the twelve Eastern and Middle; in 1860 they had risen to 30 per cent upon them. They had increased upon the Eastern and Middle $93,121,526 in relative value, or 31.3 per cent upon their ratio in 1850.

The force and fairness of the following comparison will be felt by those who know the respective conditions and capabilities of the States concerned. In 1850 the aggregate population of Ohio, Indiana and Illinois, was 2,820,215,—their aggregate wealth in real and personal property, $862,641,390,—their manufactures in the year, $98,805,983. In 1860, their products were valued at 225 millions,—increase 127.5 per cent. In 1850 the population of Maryland, Virginia, and Georgia, was 2,910,880,—their aggregate wealth $985,344,160, or, reduced by the value of their 944,578 slaves, it was $701,970,760, their manufactures of that year were valued at $69,269,614. In 1860 these products had risen to $107,776,000,—increase 55.5 per cent.

One other method of illustrating the progress of the Western States in manufacturing enterprise offers itself:—

The population of the twelve New England and Middle States in 1860, was 11,468,513; of the Western, 10,445,580. The aggregate capital wealth of the New England and Middle States was 6,298½ millions of dollars,—their manufactures of the year 1,298 millions,—equal to 20.6 per cent of their capital wealth. They had increased their capital wealth 86.6 per cent in the decade. The eleven Western States increased their capital wealth in the same time from 1,350½ to 4,519 millions, or 234.6 per cent. Much of this wealth, however, lay in valuation, latent, and incapable of employment in manufacturing production of any kind. Much of it was in the spontaneous enhancement of the value of lands yielding nothing,—capital *in posse*, not *in esse*. The New England and Middle States also had a considerable portion of such capital in expectancy and inconvertible for present uses. Assuming that the wealth available in enterprises of converting industry, should be taken to have advanced in equal ratio, the capital of the Western States, enhanced by an accretion upon the valuation of 1850 of 86.6 per cent, would give the true comparative amount for 1860. It would be 2,519½ millions, on which capital sum their products of that year would have been equal to 15.47 per cent. This estimate throws out of the comparison the market price of the uncultivated lands of Michigan, Minnesota, Kansas, Nebraska, Missouri, and Kentucky especially, and of the other five States generally, but still leaves enough of such unproductive values in the estimate to balance those of the New England and Middle States. It excludes only that portion of the spontaneous enhancement of values included in the census appraisement, which exceeds the ratio of the older States, and has the effect of putting 2,000 of the 4,519 millions to the account of increase not produced by the direct application of capital and industry.

We have reached the surprising conclusion that the manufactures of the Western States are in value to their capital effective for such use as 15.47 is to 20.6 in the great manufacturing region of the Union, or very exactly three-fourths of the proportion of product to total wealth in those States of the Atlantic slope, so much older, wealthier, denser in population, and inherently less capable of that agricultural prosperity which might well be thought likely to win away the people of the Western States from this field of competition.

To meet prevalent opinions as to the facts, and accepted theories as to what the facts should be, we offer the corroboration found in the amounts of Internal Revenue collected from these two classes of States in the fiscal year ending June 30th, 1864.

Internal Revenue from Manufactures and Productions.

The eleven Western States	paid $27,660,397=38.2 per cent.	
" twelve New England and Middle	" 44,589,687=61.7	"

Our estimate puts the manufactures of the Western States at exactly three-fourths of those of the New England and Middle in proportion to capital. The taxes paid by these States in 1864 reduces the proportion to considerably over three-fifths, but it must be observed that the values of the articles taxed are not given. Where the duties are *ad valorems* in the Commissioner's Report, the values may be calculated, but they are in so large proportion specific that this resource fails us. Moreover, the specific duties are higher on the special manufactures of the East than of the West. The products of the West are to a large extent taxed in the East, as in the case of slaughtered animals, and among other things $1,884,590 of this difference is made up by the tax on petroleum, a substance which was not in the market as a manufacture in 1860.

Beside all this, the productions of manufactures of smaller value and more widely scattered escape the assessor to a greater extent, than where they are longer established and on a larger scale.

We therefore take this very fair approximation of the internal revenue receipts to the figures reached by the process here adopted, as strongly corroborative of the results before attained. The lower result is, however, quite sufficient for our purpose, and, after cautioning the reader to take these calculations for the comparative, but not the total, value of the manufactures of the two groups of States, exhibited here only for the purpose of measuring the enterprise of the Western States by the scale of the Eastern, we proceed to draw the practical conclusions to which our inquiry points.

International Trade.

We have seen that our non-manufacturing customers took in 1860, by direct exchange, six-tenths of our purely agricultural exports, how much more by the indirect route of our European mediums of commerce we have not attempted to ascertain, but the addition would be large if it were thoroughly traced. These customers are chiefly the people of the American continent and adjacent islands in the Atlantic and Pacific oceans, and they are all inhabitants of climates north or south of us, naturally incapable of such commodities as we send them. It is also to be remarked that of less than forty millions of manufactures exported, they gave us a market for nearly thirty-two millions, or quite eight-tenths of the whole. The imports from them amounted to 153½ millions, and the half of this value under the tariff of 1857 paid duties in our ports. Their sugar, coarse wool, and tobacco paying 24 per cent; rates as high as those upon the iron, cotton and woolen manufactures of Europe. Scarcely any of their staples, except coffee, tea, and dye stuffs, were admitted free of duty. Nothing in legislation favored this trade, yet they sent us seven-sixteenths of all our imports that year. This trade exists by virtue of the natural law which rules the commerce of diverse climates and capabilities,—the law which commands exchanges for the mutual supply of those commodities in which the parties are respectively deficient. It is legitimate, because it is necessary, and depends upon no conditions for reciprocity of benefits. Mr. Mill in his "Commerce Defended," says, "The commerce of one country with another is, in fact, merely an extension of that division of labor by which so many benefits are conferred upon the human race. In the world at large one province is favorable to the production of one species of accommodation, and another to another: by their mutual intercourse they are enabled to sort and distribute their labor as most peculiarly suits the genius of each particular spot."

The conditions of trade required by the natural law, thus so well stated, apply in all circumstances to the commerce in commodities of which the respective parties have the natural monopoly,—but it is not by any means true or absolute as between nations of similar climates, capabilities, and genius for industrial enterprise. It is unquestionable that a nation of even the highest prospective capabilities, while yet in its infancy, thinly peopled, and with little material and mental capital, is greatly benefited, while such limitation of ability lasts, and in the degree in which it exists, by exchanging its coarser, cheaper, and less remunerative products with more advanced communities, for such as they will in time be able to produce for themselves; the condition of inferiority in the meanwhile imposing upon them all its attendant burdens; among which are, the vast cost of transportation, the profits of intermediates, fluctuations in demand, and the necessity of yielding to the superior the power to fix the price of both their own raw products and that of the manufactures received in exchange, with all the difference that there is between the rewards of skilled and unskilled labor against them, besides. A people capable of, and advancing toward, the highest rank, must take care that their trade shall be only *supplementary*, and graded truly to their several stages of advancement toward industrial independence. If they would be self-respecting and self-preserving, they must understand that true economy is not a matter of prices or nominal values; not a huckstering policy of buying and selling, but a science of *productive power.*

The Western States, whose condition and progress we have endeavored to display, must, sooner or later, and the sooner the better, take care to diversify their industries and provide a home-market for their abounding agriculture, or they will expose themselves to those fluctuations of prices and of demand, which have more than once driven them to burning their corn for fuel for want of a better paying market.

The European market for their surplus breadstuffs and provisions, as we have seen, is simply contemptible at best, and at all times uncertain, depending as it does for any accidental relief it may afford, upon the contingencies of foreign wars of great magnitude and long continuance, upon the occurrence of famines or general failures of crops throughout Europe, and upon the still less certain and constant ability of the masses of their people to purchase; while, on the other hand, the natural market of the American continent and the tropical regions generally, is ours by the fixed laws of climate and production, and the resulting security of exchanges; this class of our customers, always needing our products, and always able to send in exchange many millions in value more than as yet we export to them.

Extension of the Monroe Doctrine to the Commerce of the Continent.

The time has come, the necessity is upon us, our security and prosperity demand the extension of the Monroe doctrine to the *commerce* of the continent. England is ready to give up empire in government for dominion in the trade of America. The only supremacy she cares for now is that of her labor. Her only fleets and forces for invasion and conquest are her mercantile vessels and her manufactures, and our defences are not in our monitors and forts, but in our Custom-houses. Political liberty and independence are not the only care of government; industrial freedom and independence are the best security for these, and all that is most worthy of living for in this world besides. It is the prime duty of every community to provide, and defend for its members all the conditions of individual prosperity which a sound policy can command.

Theories manufactured by the master commercial nations, and designed to hold their old time colonies in industrial vassalage, must not be allowed to override universal experience. Universal, we say, for it is proved in the history of the past, that no nation has risen to the rank of a first-rate power in politics or war, in commerce or wealth, that has not studiously and persistently diversified its industries to its utmost capacity. England herself is one of the best among the examples. France and Germany are relatively as prominent; and Portugal and Turkey prove it as well by the exhaustion they have suffered from abandoning the policy of self-protection, or self-defence, against foreign invasion of their labor markets at home. As to the much vaunted Anglo-French treaty of commerce, made in 1860, which free-traders are accustomed to claim as a partial advance of their doctrine, it is demonstrable that it is quite as protective of the home industry of France, and more effectively framed for that purpose, than the Morrill Tariff, of March, 1861, was for the United States. The authorities abroad have not given up the struggle, but they have abandoned the hope of extending their doctrine of free-trade among the nations. The "London Economist" of 17th of December, 1864, concedes that its "creed is not only stationary, but retrograding," adding that, "in America, (meaning the United States,) the Canadas, Australia, and the Anglo-Saxon colonies generally, the belief in protection seems to have acquired a new vitality. The Northern Americans have raised their tariff to figures, which but for the vast war expenditure, would almost extinguish trade; the Canadians try to meet every fresh expense by raising some duty on an import, and a parliament has just been elected in Victoria pledged to introduce a system of general protection for colonial industry. Nothing is to be imported which can possibly be made, and manufacturers are to be encouraged to make, by the imposition of excessive duties upon all European goods which compete, or may compete, with local productions."

The author, after a very candid though incomplete statement of the argument on which the Australian colonists rest the policy which they have adopted, concludes, "we confess we cannot quite see the immediate remedy for this state of affairs, and are inclined to believe that patience is the only remedy."

No doctrine or dogma exposed to the test of experience, needs patience more than the one self-styled free-trade, because it starts upon the false pretence of a misnomer, and never dares venture far enough from its base of supplies to win a victory in the field of trial and hold it. Its mission of universal philanthropy would be better described as a system of free *foreign* trade, with industry at home in hand-cuffs. It means—open the ports of the world and the markets which they guard, to the exclusive traffic of the strongest, at the expense of destroying all the rival labor of the purchasing nation, and starving the workmen of the producing nation.

In the natural order of things, the free-traders will have to wait, as the world waited upon England, until protection had served its purpose, and would have been an absurdity and a nullity, if longer continued. Their tariff duties were in effect repealed by their supremacy in commerce, long before it was done by act of Parliament, and they must wait upon the Australian, Canadian, and other Anglo-Saxon colonists, who are still at the mercy of England's larger and cheaper capital, better organized machinery and cheaper wages, until these struggling people have got on even ground, and are ready for a free fight for their lives.

Setting aside theories of commerce which neither require nor tolerate any reference to history or facts, it may be asked why England, Wales, and the lowlands of Scotland, with a less area than Pennsylvania and West Virginia in the east, or Missouri alone in the West, and having neither more nor better iron and coal than either of them, and with vastly inferior food-producing power, and equally inferior command of all the supporting resources of the highest forms of industry, should nevertheless hold the commerce of the United States in their hands, make our clothing, machinery, agricultural implements, and our railroads, leaving us for our own share of mechanic labor, little besides house building other than iron structures, horse-shoeing, the printing of local items, and grave digging, which of necessity must be done on the spot?

The one sole reason why England obtained the mastery of the ocean, and command of the world's business is, that she exported no raw material; and the reason why the Southern States went into ruin by the route of rebellion is, because they exported nothing else. The trade of Germany at the beginning of the century was hides, tallow, flax, and wool exported, for cloth and cutlery in return, and Bonaparte could make their territory his fighting ground. Since the battle of Waterloo, they have been making their own clothes and cutlery, and his nephew, with more resources and stronger alliances, was obliged to keep within the line of war with Austria, which the rest of Germany prescribed.

The Western States,

as we have seen, showed a surprising advance in manufacturing and mechanic industry before the rebellion, and have doubtless greatly added to it during the war. Not only indirectly but directly it has become an *important interest of their own, and the opening of the wilderness beyond them will soon* make them Eastern States both in position and policy. Ohio, the oldest of them, has already had some admonitory experience. Her rate of increase in population in the decade, 1850–60, was but 18.14 per cent, while Pennsylvania made an increase of 25.71, New York 25.29, and New Jersey 37.27 per cent. She has been losing relative weight in Congress and in the Electoral College, as against Pennsylvania, and now that peace is restored, and an ebb-tide of emigration from the older to the newer States west of the Mississippi has set in with unprecedented volume and force, she immediately, with Indiana and Illinois, ere long, and all the others in their turn, will have to look to the policy which secures the growth of communities by securing the greatest variety and the largest profits of industry.

More than once in our past history, an overwhelming flood of foreign manufactures has driven the capital and labor of the East into competition with the chief industry of the West, and its products have forthwith fallen to half their ordinary value, and afterwards declined to nothing. If experience can teach anything it proves that it is better to have ten millions of eastern purchasers consuming a hundred millions of their products, than half as many rivals thrown into their own field of production.

But the mischief of a system destructive of home manufactures, is not by any means confined to the food-growing interest of the West. Among the many things for which the trans-oceanic world can give them no market—such as lumber, cattle provender of all kinds, live stock, all sorts of green crops, mutton, poultry, and the other immense values that will not bear distant transportation, there is an interest of practically unlimited value deserving special attention:—

Wool.

If the manufacturing nations *can* give us a market for this product, will any one undertake to show why, for a dozen years together, they never took above twenty thousand dollars worth in any one year, nor so much as this in the average of those years? Our European market for this article, deserves no more respectful statement than that it does not pay for the playing cards imported from them. The very tabular statements of the Treasury Department grin contempt upon this "export" of ours, just as the history of its fortunes at home glares at the policy which has hitherto ruled it.

The increase of the live stock of the Western States in the last census decade, including sheep, was 143½ per cent. The increase of the sheep themselves was just $2\frac{7}{10}$ per cent! But their quality must have improved a little, and the very best of them have somehow escaped the butcher-shop, for the clip of 1860 exceeded in weight that of 1850 seventeen per cent, in the face of an average increase of every other agricultural product in those States of $125\frac{6}{10}$ per cent. Under the policy of that period, the cloth manufacturers were crushed out of existence, and the farmer found no sufficient market for his wool, either at home or abroad. He was just then, as he thought, "buying his cloth cheap," but he was not "selling his wool dear;" on the contrary he was sending his sheep to the shambles.

Somebody in the direction of affairs when this wretched policy was adopted, must have blundered; somebody may have been telling the constituency that the protection of home manufactures, and of the resulting home market for the hundred-fold forms of farm produce which can never go abroad, was "class legislation," and that it made imported iron, cloth and cutlery dear; forgetting, or not knowing, that the provider of food and raw materials, is as much a manufacturer himself, as the weaver, the puddler, or the smith who gives the last turn in the process of converting them into commodities for use, and is as much a partner in the business and its profits. Forgetting, also, that even if the foreigner will or can give the farmer a market, he would be all the better for having two, and one of them at home and at hand.

The war and its incidents shed a flood of light upon the effect of a well secured home consumption for agricultural products of every kind, of which the wool-growing interest is an example. In the ten years before the rebellion, the sheep of Pennsylvania had decreased 12 per cent in number. In May, 1864, the Agricultural Bureau reports an increase of 76 per cent in four years. In Illinois they had fallen off in the last census decade 14 per cent. In the first two years of the war, according to the report of the county assessors, they had increased from 769,135 to 1,206,695, and the editor of the *Chicago Tribune*, estimates the number at 3,000,000 at the close of the year 1864—an increase of 290 per cent in four years. This immense advance is owing simply to a protective tariff, aided by the high rate of foreign exchange and absolute possession of the home market.

Conclusions.

The Western States are already the heart of the nation. They keep the gate of the future. They are much more than a balance of power now. The Empire of the Union is possible to them. But they must take care of themselves. They must meet their responsibilities to the nation. They must take themselves out of the category of "Our Anglo-Saxon colonies." They must find a shorter route from the mouth of the Mississippi to South America, than by way of Liverpool; and, they may, also, as well understand that they are nearer than New York is to the Rocky Mountains. They must shape their policy toward industrial independence. They must secure to themselves every form of labor which their infinite variety of capability demands; or, they will hang their peace of mind and pecuniary prospects upon the Atlantic telegraph that threatens to put Liverpool, Halifax and Chicago, into a commercial circuit with its preposterous *centre* and governing battery at the eastern end.

19

[illegible] In the years before the rebellion the decrease of [illegible] cattle had increased 12 per cent [illegible]. In May 1891 the Agricultural Bureau reported an increase of 70 per cent in four years, [illegible] the last census [illegible] cent. In the [illegible] two years [illegible] according to the report of the [illegible] they had [illegible] [illegible] and the [illegible] the [illegible] of the [illegible] increase of 300 per cent in [illegible] years. This [illegible] [illegible]

www.ingramcontent.com/pod-product-compliance
Lightning Source LLC
LaVergne TN
LVHW011145110826
845150LV00008B/2525

* 9 7 8 1 4 1 8 1 9 2 4 8 8 *